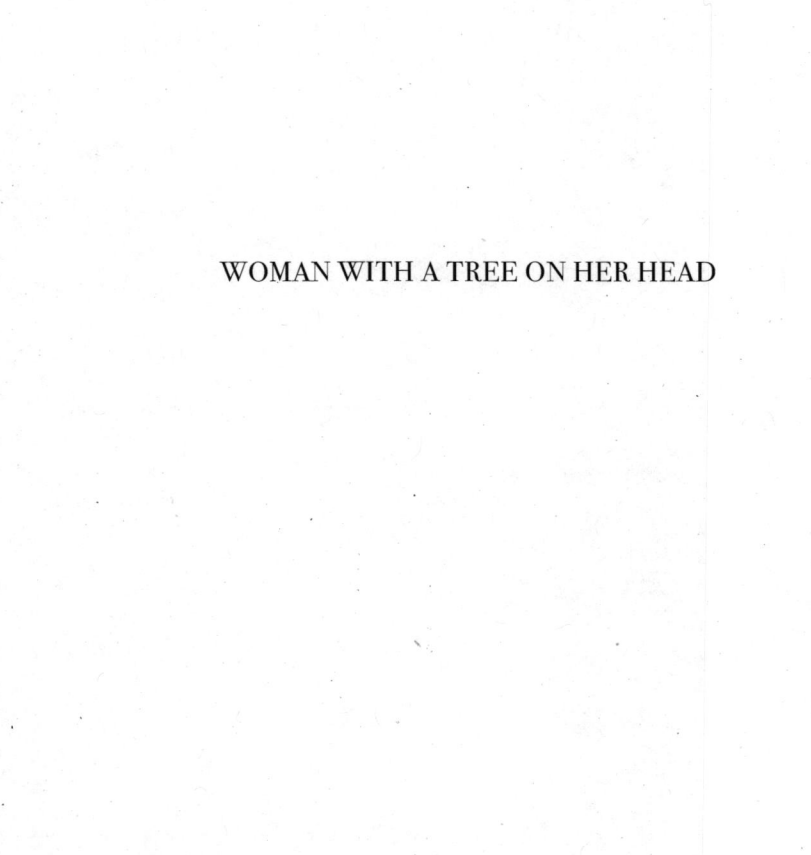

WOMAN WITH A TREE ON HER HEAD

WOMAN WITH A TREE ON HER HEAD

poems PATRICIA CORBUS

Acknowledgments

Many thanks to the following publications, in which these poems appeared:

The Chariton Review: "De Colores", "I Visit My Husband's Grave at the Veterans Cemetery."

The Coe Review: "She Looks Back."

Confrontation: "Requiem."

Cottonwood: "How Quickly", "Leaving the Day of the Dead."

The Fiddlehead: "The Bright Blue Sofa."

Nimrod Journal: "Under the Mulberry Tree."

Notre Dame Review: "La Vie en Orange."

Poetry East: "Elegy for a Sailor", "My Trip to Italy", "Space Odyssey."

South Carolina Review: "Nebula through Telescope."

Western Humanities Review: "Homage to St. Introvert."

Copyright 2023 © Patricia Corbus

Book Design: Melissa J White
Set in Adobe Caslon Pro

ISBN: 979-8-9854357-1-9

All Rights Reserved

Blue Edge Books
Santa Fe, NM

Contents

The Bright Blue Sofa	11
Clouds Shaped Like Waves	12
Under the Mulberry Tree	14
Ode to Her	15
In the Jasper Palace	16
Condolence	17
In the Gila Desert	18
Advice for a Baby	19
With the Learned Poets	20
My Trip to Italy	22
In the Stream	23
Valerie at the Hippodrome	24
The Heaven Tree	25
Ste. Delisse and the Cold Water	26
What She Did	27
Listen	28
Requiem	29
Space Odyssey	30
Waiting	31
A Trip in the Dark	32
Leaving the Day of the Dead	33
The Oracle	34
De Colores	35
Going to the Fair	37
Flying by Night	38
Elegy for a Sailor	39
A Courtyard in Morelia	40
Lake Michigan Blues	41
What If?	43
Orange Jasmine	44
That Baby	45
Giant Red Bird	46

Once the World	47
She Remembers	48
Homage to St. Introvert	49
I Wish I Could	50
What it Was	51
The String	52
Nebula through Telescope	54
At the End of the Day	55
Hotel Splendide	56
Petal, Clay, Ice	57
She Looks Back	58
How Quickly	59
Islander	60
Stairway for a Demiurge	61
The Poetry Reading	62
Le Jardin de Picpus	63
I Visit my Husband's Grave at the Veterans Cemetery	64
La Vie en Orange	65
Woman with a Tree on her Head	66

for Burt in the farsighted blue

The Bright Blue Sofa

        My life, a streaked peach,
fell into a light blue haze of snakes
and smoky journeys never ended
or begun, collapsed into a pit of stone
wrapped in a coat of snow – and when
the snow melted and the stone cracked,
there was the same bright blue sofa

on the lawn under a banner in the sky,
*We Know Everything, But Not When
It Will Happen.* The sofa is still quite
comfortable, though it has constricted
into a loveseat, I mean a chair, I mean
a stick, a twig, and the yards around me
are dark, and oceans lap at my feet.

Clouds Shaped Like Waves

I

The sun, a gelid gold,
    the lake, a nearsighted blue.
        —I'm afraid
that art has nothing to do
with my story, and the end
has already happened.

II

Even the darkest stars become antsy,
begin to itch, wiggle, feel hot,
and then spasms begin—sparks,
convulsions, explosions.
Something is coming alive.
        —Entirely natural,
say the good ghosts, nothing more
than can be expected.
The green arms of the corn wave
Goodbye! Goodbye! He's coming!
The portal is opening.

III

My cloak, once cloth-of-gold,
    gleaming and costly, has turned

    to ashes falling about
my shoulders, yet I know no

    color more costly, more honest
        or elegant, than charcoal.

This rich burden of darkness
    I carry so lightly that I glide over

    vast oceans of illusion
like light skating in from a far star.

IV

Back to now,
up to no
good, and soon
to be out
of sight like
you behind the
tracery of bare
cold branches, I
suddenly see you
high on a
branch, this side
of infinity, waving,
your long legs
dangling in khaki
pants from Joe
Sugar's. Ha, I
cry, feeling your
arms around me.

Under the Mulberry Tree

The sun's warm hand swept over her, scattering
    formless lights over the world of forms.
        She was thinking about the colossal space
between bits of matter, all that elbow room
    for change, making it possible to tease open,

        even reinterpret, long-finished events.
Everyone's future is happy because it hasn't
    happened yet, she thought—the organ grinder
        may laugh at finding four mulberries in his
little monkey's cap, and the horseman,

    hurrying by, may yet dismount to gather me
        into his cloak. —A horned owl hovers—
blinks a yolk-yellow eye, and flaps away—
    inside the solar wind, inside the moment,
            particles whirling, on the wing.

Ode to Her

When the creature attacks, that pit bull
who gave psychology such a stink in the suburbs,
I know my small power more pure, narrower all the time,
know hers is fat as air, fast as any thunderclap,
booming a kind of killing kindness
which chases into new hunts and byways,
smells blood and bumps me off my way.

The woman has no sense of humor, only teeth
to shake and tear tender underarm and belly flesh.
She startles the very outcroppings from old family
volcanoes into wild red rivers flowing again—
heaved into such crematoriums of the spirit,
who would not melt and run away?

But I am mutinous and tired of excesses,
tired of being vast, seeing everyone's point of view,
ready for the intermittent flashlight beam
that is mine alone, and no one else's.
Sick of right and left, their sour washcloth smells.
So Enemy, Teacher, I smile at you
as if you were old nanny Estralita saying
Piss of cake with a blob of endive in your teeth.

Big broody mother with decals of cross, ankh, crescent
moon and star, you-name-it, Elmered on your leathery back,
I hold you down with my tiny but willing heel,
and drive my own hook deep into your murderous jaw.

In the Jasper Palace

Scheherazade and the Vizier keep on playing
For their lives; they talk about not failing.
Night is coming. Look at winter sailing
Shadows on the wall—What am I saying?

For their lives, they talk about not failing.
The moon is searching for her dear lost master.
Shadows on the wall, what am I saying?
The cards are falling faster, faster.

The moon is searching for her dear lost master.
In torn pantaloons she walks, almost awake.
The cards are falling faster, faster.
A mistaken star has plunged into the lake.

In torn pantaloons she walks, almost awake.
The story that she tells begins with *No*.
A mistaken star has plunged into the lake.
Such histories are not uncommon, and so

The story that she tells begins with *No*.
An owl is robbing nests, hounds are baying.
Such histories are not uncommon—and so
Scheherazade and the Vizier keep on playing.

Condolence

The first one said, "My dear, it is what it is.
    Life's a kindergarten for souls.
            He'll always live in your heart."
I said, "Thanks! Now I know he's safe
        in God's breast pocket."

And the second one hugged me, saying,
    "Everything happens for a reason.
        He's in a better place."
And I cried, "Bless you for that!
    Now I see him orbiting the earth,
        looking everywhere for me."

    The third one, spiritual, but not religious,
took my hand and said, "He's all around you
        in nature, the great healer.
Cast positive energy into the universe,
    go through the allotted five stages,
        and move on."

    (O, Abelard, Juliet, Orpheus, why
did you arrive too early for this sweet dogma!)

    So I said, "Because of you, kind souls,
I hear acorns hitting my tin roof
    and I see cattails like corn-dogs swaying,

    a goldfinch
        hiding in the earth's shadow—
and a dreaming bear in a cold cave
    about to open hazel eyes."

In the Gila Desert

Considering her barren geology,
Dry as a yucca and tired of barbs,

She willed her voice to say,
"Stop whining *Is This My Home?*

My REEAL Home? Because it isn't
And it is. Whiteoak and Blackwater

Are everywhere—the darkest hole
Is wound with sun, the whitest oak

A welter of blackest water. Every
Story runs *Stars, No Stars, Stars,*

Sun, No Sun, Sun. You are home, stay
Or leave as you will." And solemnly,

She slowly bowed her head upon
The ground—her bloom was that heavy.

Advice for a Baby

Mommy is a lot more than Mommy. Daddy, too.
    Those bobble-heads around you contain multitudes.
You'll grow. Don't get stuck in something too little.

Everything expands. Watch the night sky roll by.
    It's okay to be positive but not at the expense of reality.
Your body is delicate and programmed to die.

A bigger world is real, too, and breaks into this one.
    Lives in it actually, if you're plucky enough to look.
Plenty of people think that things are easier than they are.

They are dangerous. Run. Wishful thinking leads
    to madness and despair, but go ahead and cry. Someone
will probably feed you. The story of your life

will mostly be the people in your life. The Creator
    loves stories. Can't help it. It's his nature. Play with words.
They are stellar winds. Fall in love with color. Do grow up.

Immaturity is cute, but maturity is beautiful. Love
    and Horror kiss, then slap each other. Eros has arrows.
Good is more real than evil. Life is hard. Have a nice time.

With the Learned Poets

1

As if a fit had passed, I recollected myself,
counted my limbs, the fingers on my hands,

saw the Wabash shake itself like a dog, breaking
into primary colors, heard birds yodeling

in twelve ways I'd never heard before,
and saw twice in the woods no bluebird,

but that smaller blue bird which is wholly blue,
the indigo bunting—and was satisfied at last

that it was about its own business and stood
for absolutely nothing—yet wondering why the one

that symbolized happiness was inconsistent, did not
go the whole way to blue, but had a muddy orange breast.

I said, *Whatever you want from me, do it.*

2

           Walt was serious,
and even I have met two or three people who were serious,
who might go the whole way, not part of the way:
persons who would not call larkspurs delphiniums
or rose campions carnations, magnolias tulips.

I am not speaking of those stump-heads who have splashed
their moxie so much that it has soaked us all.

I am sick of their autobiographies, all those plastic
poinsettias. Please stop telling me about your divorce.

I want to hear how you were stung in the womb
toward oblivion, how the smudged sunset is pulling you
like an undertow over the edge, which is to say—
    Do you even want to go all the way?

3

White stuff floats
through rain-trees.
Whitish bubbles pop
on the creamy green pond.
How artfully
seeds get themselves
germinated and broadcast.
If I were a cardinal
this is where I'd want to live.

4

The town contracted to a tight smile,
all green and mild, gewgaws and the smell of junk shops,
that acrid smell that means things are eating
their own bodies. How cleverly they announce their need
              to be burned or buried.
That tent on the lawn looks like a funeral about to begin.
Something in me has ended. Some false hope back-flipped
              and splashed into the pond.
All I can hear is the honking of geese around me.
    I kick my foot at their bulging necks.

My Trip to Italy

Strumpets and dignitaries
    pinched my watch and my bottom
        on the way to the valley of hell—
all that sulfur and lava, shrieks and oaths
    as Capri floated by upon the waters

        like underwear, and across the straits
where tectonic plates once shook Messina
    so hard that her memory fell out,
        Etna smoked thoughtfully over my head.
Dante stepped out of the fumes, took

    my hand, and hurried me back to Rome
        just in time for us to close
Keats' eyes, warm ourselves in his face,
    and clatter into exile over the roof of hell,
        our arms full of red roses.

In the Stream

Death in stars so beautiful,

the Ring Nebula ejecting

its outer layers into space,

as our curtains open to welcome

the magician who smiles

and never tells how, but hints

when we look steadily away

from his hands. Here is the action—

our ejecta, color, abstraction,

release, streaming like the sunset.

The universe is in its teens

of billions. When it ejects

a tipsy boat, shall we not take it?

Valerie at the Hippodrome

So there it was. Her feet could no longer sashay.
Her ankles were too dense, Chinook-
Driven, too thick to waft a lemon verbena sachet.

For sure, Cynic, that sentence was intense, its gothic
Elements too vast for a bosomy Rudy Friml valse,
Too fast for any buckwheat ballet, its antique hook

Of sense, to all intents, locked with chits in sweaty vaults
Where an agile python plotted his plots—knotted
Twisted, rapid canards and somersaults,

As well as a few not so beau erotic jests. Val, besotted
By plonk, in a louche manner spread
Her fair hair & wept into her pumps, her sequins rattled.

—Say you so, Beefy? In her greeny heart she's pledged
Death to the Horned Rams of Black Lake Hellfire Rollerball.
While tittering mice waltz in your head, O Vapid,

Hear her diamond lariat whip & crack the mirrored ball.

The Heaven Tree
In memory of Amon

A tree blooming clusters
    of pink and gold drew me
        into the long dark park.
How can a tree bloom both
    dull, immortal gold
        and tender, naked pink?
—Then I remember you
    I slighted, who died young,

    who once said to me,
*You look fresh as
    a clump of pink flowers.*
        And I wanted to see you
again so much that I ran
    toward the hidden tree,
        its flowers hovering
above, too high to see,

    faster, faster, until
        I knew that if I lived
forever, sprouting golden
    flowers in eternal light,
        I would still have to bear
pumping out urgent pink
    blooms of human romance
        in mortal despair.

Ste. Delisse and the Cold Water

It must be cold, it must be clear,
must be written in, have inner meaning,
must grow, must pour over the saints and monsters
we so need to attain philosophy, that lying hag.

Pour it over her head, that sweet Delisse
    whose simple habit is duck egg blue,
        her panties dead mouse gray.

But touch her not, mortal fool.
She must be leapt over, gone to seed.
You must fire her proper, go to school,
graduate with honor. You must be cold, cruel.

Throw her out of the house.
    Then leave yourself.
        No one's panties are dead mouse gray.

What She Did

She picked herself up like a bag of corn
    leaking its contents, and when she looked back,
        there was a long, golden trail.
She picked herself up like a table,
        two legs broken off, staggering
  under its awkwardness,
    and when she looked back,
        two footprints marched right up to her.
She picked herself up like a river
    following the thread that physics supplied,
  and when she glanced out toward the sea,
        there was a lariat
        flying silver droplets around her head.
She picked herself up like a planet
        rolling in her arms, struggling
  to carry it to some unknown ellipsis,
    and when she was about to be pulled back,
        she saw herself as one who tends the stars.
She picked herself up like a universe,
    all there was and ever would be,
        too big for love or sorrow,
  put her ear close to it, listened
    to something like imagined music,
        and threw it like a shell back into the dark sea.
She picked herself up like a baby
        fresh from her own womb,
  and held herself close to her body,
        feeling its life flow into hers,
    like the spirits of Corn and River, like a Planet
        traveling around its mother,
      passing, but always pulled back,
        like the Universe gobbling space,
like the Baby, swimming in its own glimmering wake.

Listen

Night is a slow pony
      poking his muzzle
            at the moon, mistaking it
for a wild, white apple.
    —Can you feel his broad,
        warm back between your thighs?

～

Before I went into exile, passing over
    Latawatah Creek and Toad Suck Park,
I scattered the path with Venetian pearls,
    and listen for their crunch under your feet.

Requiem

I'm reading about loss and time since there's
    nothing else to think of, much less read about,
        what with the light bulb flickering

and the peaches in the can about to explode.
    Yet there's chili in the refrigerator, tires go

        round and round, and water wanders in
and out of the bayou, mumbling its favorite word,
voluble. I'm a flashback myself, stretched out

        on a brown leatherette sofa.
Happiness is nothing, compared to the intimacy

    of loss—it fills everything up, you drown in it.
        A Yellow Cab is coming, and my bag
is packed—evening dress, strappy heels, eye drops,

    pictures in my purse of the floating continents
        and their peoples—everyone ready

to ride and not minding it much, since we're
    the planet's own products and outpourings,
        carrying around our own atmosphere

wherever we go, like nectar or sweat. Don't forget
    to water the prayer plant. Don't write.

Space Odyssey

That black hole in your iris
blasts matter—where?
and those epaulets on your shoulders?
—bullets of course.
Where could you not toboggan?
What could you not say—
I'm here! I'm home! I'm gone!
The power of those eyes,
even these letters, circling, curling around you,
ejecting—what?
Please let me hear from you.
Slip a letter under my door,
smoke an exploding cigar with me,
take me out for a cherry bomb
or a Molotov cocktail.
          —You,
the one, the o, the dot, the whole—
my transport, my peace.

Waiting

When they closed the lid on me
my very bones of benevolence
                were glowing,
so I smiled, listening
     to comforting mumbles
               and sentimental moans
like telephone wires singing
                 sweet dirges.
Sometimes a few cackles broke out
    about godhead
             and maidenhead,
 though not one fresh egg was laid.
My feet were cold.
             Feeling a bit
    of post-mortem depression,
I listened, glad to be gone,
     waiting for the sequel,
            the guide, the signal,
some huge gong to strike
         and reverberate me home.
Still waiting, I pushed open the lid,
            walked home with you,
and here I am—
            looking out of your eyes,
lying in your bed,
     listening to your CPAP machine,
waiting for Mama
      to come kiss me goodnight,
and for Papa to wake me up, crying,
            Rise and shine!

A Trip in the Dark

She carried a green lantern, its cresset
    peeping out like a moon's egg.

    The Hired Boy, his arm under hers,
escorted her like a ship, guiding her

    to Navarre, the tiptop land between
        Spain and France, lost empire Tir-na-nog,

crow's nest of the North Star.
    No man-of-war with a coat of arms,

    but a farm boy with dirty sleeves,
he whispered in her ear, as they brushed

    through trees, rough boughs
        that in the morning would be too red

to be pink, too pink to be red. *Watch out,*
    my lady, for logs and frogs in the dark,

    for falling wasps and stars. No way
could you get there safe, no way,

    without my strength and purity. He kissed
        her forehead. *That was close,* they cried,

falling to the forest floor like feathers.

Leaving the Day of the Dead

The peace lily's cobra head turned
to follow us as we spoke of sorrow

and regret, smiling. We were not burned
by the sunset's desperate red, chilled

by the woodpecker's demented laugh,
or spooked by the bald cypress's sudden

full head of green hair. Three of us dead,
and one dying, arm in arm, we walked

into a sandy lake where the moon floated
on its back, shivering the water.

Mortal magic had crumbled with the sun.
       The world was spinning

her wool into the last few feathers
of sunset. We began to breathe and splash

each other, startling a lone loon sleeping
on the moon's belly, and watched it push off

for home through looms, pinwheels,
          pinpricks of stars.

The Oracle

But why this yearning for hand-hewn stones,
the heraldic arch, the uncut jewel, cloaks,
forests and horses, houses isolate and complete
with talking birds in tall cages, slack-

jawed villagers, arrows in their quivers,
a stone altar the color of gulls, surrounded
by herbs and foraging pigs, the fertile crescent
moon, a shout of light from invisible lips—

when, in the lake outside my window, fish
circle slowly on their sides, gills up, and you
speak quietly to me on the phone, your lungs
filling, your voice the voice of the raccoons

who invade this yard at night—falling stars
with a rattle on the end. In the giant's house
sunlight hardly ever reaches the floor, and when
it does, its icicles are razor-sharp to the touch,

scattering and sliding like minnows across cold
green marble. Will the lips of oracles never
stop babbling doom? Even now I see their deadly-
voluptuous king, hear the beaten gold of his voices.

De Colores

Blue cries out for gold to enter it,
but sighs with relief when gold leaves
its cobalt pure, undefiled, able to sleep.
Orange is smart, wants to go far
in the world without losing its soul.
Pink is a weak sister without the infusion
of some friend, blue or yellow, to render it fresh,
the something new and different it craves.
Salmon swims around in its breeding costume.
Puce is an English flea drowned in a thimble.
Green, artificial and bright as turf,
weary of symbolism, would like
to be simple and decent, but can't.
Brown, ashamed but proud,
wears pine trunks, is background,
pronounces *natural* distinctly, clearly,
without clearing its throat.
Chartreuse is a color with a smell, heady
with French, liquorish, ecclesiastical overtones.
Purple lies like a prayer rug. Pretentious,
violent introvert that she is, not giving much,
but getting everything,
like the adorable child she isn't.
Roll black over you and rest.
Pull yellow over you and yell *hallelujah,*
filled with corn, wheat, ivory,
your chest pumping torrents of triumphal.
Pull white over you and see again
the world through eggshell.
Royal personages of many moods
and temperaments, colors float
in reflecting pools, ride scattered waves

on the Luz River, and have the run
of the jungle king's jungle.

Going to the Fair

I walk a trough of shallow green past
    a door spiked round with gladiolas tall
        as the eaves, past the scarred beech, origin
of the word *book,* and look, there's the high ride,
echoing the beech's branches' undulations,

all the people screaming a mosquito drone,
    bobbling slowly along the branches, but fast
        if you're actually inside the gondolas
that shine so smartly red. —And there you are,
your eyes bark-brown above the crowd.

I will never let you go, inveterate marauder.
    Even if you fell from the tiny cars, rolling
        into the water, I would catch you, even
if you weren't there, and if God declined
to relinquish you, I would climb back

into the gray, scarred bark, rise with its sap
    to the highest leaf and leap into the fall air.
        Only your presence could make me bear
your loss. Get me out of this dark fair.
Home is where you are. *Take me there.*

Flying by Night

I am quiet now, used to death
        and the plane's stutter,
                the clouds like bruised fists,

patient with flights over cornfields
        on stormy nights, the ones I want most
                tucked in their long beds.

In ancient Chinese "wind and rain"
        is a delicate euphemism for sex,
                but I feel earth's distress.

How glad I am
        that I see nothing more than the cornfield
                thinking wet thoughts

now that the rain has ended,
        no longer longing for the sun
                but for the cold mouth of the moon.

Elegy for a Sailor

                    Here on shore
we watch things come and go.
    Every day water and sky
        make love on the clouds.
                Giant water blooms
expand violently over our heads,
   float and float away.
          Shaken by such a ruckus,
no wonder we bloom and fade—
     morning glories wakened by dawn,
         petals torn off by noon.
The wind is rising,
          but sunset also rises,
    like gardenia pollen
or a coral reef releasing its vast desires.
         Though our sun has sailed,
    leaving a wake like a pathway home,
what's left of its light
            makes our faces shine.
          We talk deep
into the night—
            and soon the moon
      out where buoys chime and roll,
   bobs like a porch light on the horizon.

A Courtyard in Morelia

We discovered you by the splashing of water
                and the din of starlings
 in a bougainvillea
        climbing red-handed over the wall.
That night three old men
     droned a drunken serenade:
             Señor, make me a portal.
The sharp smell of drains, then flowers.
       —You thought I said that a statue
of the Infant of Prague in a dim alcove
was the "infinite frog,"
              but even as we laughed,
   Child and Frog fused
to help the Man of Fire break through cement
        and guide us north to Guanajuato,
              the place of frogs,
bypassing Lent, revolution, and drunkenness,
        to that one place
your father prepared for us sixty years ago—
    before we knew how time kills,
              stands still,
then darts out of the shadows
           to rescue and restore.

Lake Michigan Blues

This lake's an ocean
        of gray and silver streaks,
an Alpine chain of clouds
            over Wisconsin.

You seem so near, so here—
    those long legs stretch out beside me,
the voices on the beach, the *sostenuto*
    of the wind in the beeches,
a many-throated chord with a growl,
    the long slide and slap of the waves.

~

The bridge across my moat is up, closed.
No one can enter my castle
        except by air, balloon or wings.
    Otherwise, stay away.
              Stop smiling at me.

~

In town, the people, florid and yellow
    in shorts, move around, grabbing
breakfast in the motels, slurping
    ice cream in the shops, buying toys,
candy, hot, milky coffee. I look in their
    faces and see Pleasure Island Pigs.
I say let them eat, fatten, squeal and die.

~

How easily the sun and moon penetrate

the forest's floor, and how easily they rise,
    leaving no spark of gold or silver.
How easily waves of fog stick to those
thick trees breathing clouds, and in the dawn
    how easily gold gilds branches
in tiny increments, and green breathes gold
back into the sky, like fire exhaling
    up a chimney.

～

No clouds. Everything horizontal
    as a flow-blue platter—the sky
over me the inside of a faded
    flow-blue teacup. I am a teacup,
the biggest piece gone. Missing.

～

I would like to be the one
to whom people tell their secrets,
the dagger in their hearts,
pulsing, convulsing, pulsing.

～

Yellow lilies nod violently
    as the wind wraps the flag
        around the pole.
—The Pole Star pulls me farther north
    to melting ice, a polar bear
        beside me on the floe
            bearing us out to sea,
a narwhal watching.

What If?

What if I opened a teashop serving teacakes and head cheese, Bûche de Noël and blood-pudding, milk and mortadella?

What if my leitmotif was three screams followed by a clash of cymbals?

What if my cat and I died at the same time and she convinced St. Peter to let me enter heaven on her own recognizance?

What if it were pleasant to be old, ugly, have no future, and be of no interest to anybody?

What if I could somehow prevent Tom Chatterton's suicide at 17 by sending him money and news that the Romantics would adore him?

What if you foolishly preferred the word languish to the word lagoon?

What if all my loved ones, even liked ones, on the other side got together and yelled so loud that I could hear what they had to say?

What if a knife in a cup symbolizes not only sex, but my cooking and most academics?

What if you heard something like a pistol shot from inside your intestines, as I once did?

What if your totem was the wind and you wore it in a locket around your neck?

Orange Jasmine

A dandelion puffball in the wind, the moon is rising
              as I watch a regatta of stars racing by

to be destroyed and made new again.
              I, always afraid, am not afraid

to ask the Cosmos, one person to another,
              not to dissolve me with all the rest

of the costumes of rank and habitude,
              but to retain some essence of my loves—

faces, hands, something said, even drops
              of my two bayous and Lake Michigan,

feathers from Elling's peacocks, drowsy
              in tall pines, their tails falling, flowing

like ancestors' beards. Remembrance
              which continues like a path electrons

might unexpectedly choose, an intuition
              leading to ecstasy, like the perfume

of my orange jasmine tree filling the night
              and our lungs, infiltrating our houses,

roaming the neighborhood,
              intoxicating our dreams.

That Baby

The baby, cheeky and cheerful,
a fistful of roses in his hand,
flies low
over a marble forest,
scattering dreams,
waking up
the dead now
beginning to move their toes
under the broken headstones.
See that knee break through?
Those hands?
That head, shattering concrete—
That smile?

Giant Red Bird

It takes prescience to puzzle the maze
and to know whether to throw stones
at the head of the giant red bird
when it rears outside the prison walk

like red thunder, the eye a lightning-
cold wheel of obsidian peering down—
or whether to use that eye as a mirror
to find some way out of the labyrinth.

But whether it plucks us up and carries
us away, its worms, or whether we drop
in the boxwood tunnels, we will be food
for something, as snowy, erotic angel eggs

laid in feathery corners are food for us.
Like all blind innocence so good to eat—
inside ferny cracks, delicious blue yolks
snore, grow wings, dream of soaring.

Once the World

Olive groves and the moving eye
    of the hurricane, the dogwood's blossom,
        a flurry of dark-eyed snowflakes.

—But I am free of all that—
    no hand to hold, no brightening eye.
        Human love, face, arms, mouth, goodbye.

I have fallen in love with the solitary earth,
    its spin, its spewing lava, cold and heat,
        the dead birds who sang to me.

I almost remember the baby voice
    of the osprey, the cardinal calling Canizzio!
        Canizzio!, cowbells clanking.

I remember everything, even what didn't happen,
    all packed inside earth's blue cloak, stuffed
        with caresses, knives, bandages.

Once the world blew a word into my ear,
    An image into my eye,
        a piece of bread into my mouth.

the word was
the image was
the bread was

something from somewhere else
    something I heard, saw, tasted and forgot
        though I live for it to come again.

Everything is survivable, even death.

She Remembers

her cousins clumping around
in Aunt Violet's high-heeled shoes,
how they'd sidle up and smirk,
     Where's your daddy?
She'd whisper in their dirty pink ears,

Rotting in the hot Florida sand,
DEAD as your own daddy will be soon—
but up here in cold, ugly North Carolina
you'll have to pile quilts on his grave
to keep him down. If they asked again,

she'd say, *French-kissing your momma,*
or *Peeing in the First Baptist Church,*
or *Just resting up, waiting to see*
what happens next, or *Getting ready*
to jam his tongue down your throat.

She knows she was not wrong
to torment those who tormented her.
Making little devils squirm still sends
her straight to heaven—and hell,
they enjoyed it more than she did.

Homage to St. Introvert

St. Introvert, palms in the air,
waited for the presence to descend,
his mind darkened into the loveliness
of any desolate, untamed mind, removed
from the castle with its knights, clergy

and pennants flapping, purveyors of right
and left performing tricks. –These are led
by St. Extrovert, who exposes himself
again and again to the crowd, his poodles
frothing and snapping among the cultivated

Dijon roses, scattering feverish dreams
among the peasants already lying so still
in the sweetsilver tangle of delicate,
untellable grief—suspicious to the bone
from having been gnawed by donkey's years

of carnivores. They smell the smell of wolf
on St. Extrovert, and know that he has come
to tear their tender hinder parts.—Yet, when
St. Introvert's prayers meet in the air
with old Elizabeth's, rising like hot ashes

from her invalid's bed, priests, jugglers,
castles, jesters disappear—and there are
only moles and voles, foxes and rabbits
around a tree, wind caught in its branches,
and the spinning egg, Earth, asleep in her nest.

I Wish I Could

catch sight of a pileated woodpecker again, or at least hear its beak going whomp whomp whomp into a tree trunk.

have an hour, even ten minutes a year, to talk on the phone to dead loved ones, though I can't imagine the conversation. How are you? Not bad. Debbie got a divorce, etc.

have a law made that one afternoon a year every house would be open for anyone to visit.

see my soul in a physical form. I think it would be surprising and complex with lots of colors and shading. Fired and unfired clay, some porcelain, bits of mica, ebony, gemstones. I'd like to hold it in my hands, turn it around, listen to its whir.

be truly, inexplicably beautiful for a day. Who knows how many Dantes would spring forth? What's better than beauty?

enter people's souls at night as they sleep. No burglary or sacrilege intended. I just want to glide around the furniture. You'd never know I was there.

like to know every color and its family personally. Ditto numbers. Climb trees again, my legs swinging high in the air,

tell you how glad I am to be mortal.

What it Was

It was the crackle of logs releasing the sun,
                wrapping us in warm parachute silk.
It was seeing the sun and the moon at the same time.
It was you, and before that, two,
                one from the past, one from the past-present.
It was St. Exupéry writing, *We are faithful members*
    of the same church, you with your customs, I with mine.
It was all those white flowers around the cottage—
                pale, imitation hibiscus, Rose of Sharon.
Strike that. It was the exploding wildflowers, touch-me-nots.
It was I, weak and ineffective
                      in the unstoppable universe.
It was you saying in my ear
              The future is a blue door.

The String

      The idea is not that this string
represents life. It flops around,
goes crooked, straight, gets dirty,
and after a while, where is it?
      This map represents the path
the string took. Beside a table
daubed with paint, woods begin

walking away to the north.
      The map itself is crumpled—
long thin diamonds drip from every
fold. But the creek beside the table
where the old folks picnic, runs green.
      The sun is a setting hen. Trees
crowd around, talking about rain, fire,

that sort of thing. The string itself
is nowhere to be found. It is not
      in my pocket. Just wild animals.
Out here, bookkeepers are popes, stern
watchers of animals. Homesteaders
on their backs look unto biggish hills.
      As for us, we correspondents

explore the country with notepads,
washing away the mind as a blush rose
is almost completely washed of burgundy.
      —Jealousy has nothing to do with it.
The high-toned spruces just refuse.
Yet what bobs to the creek's surface
is a creamy path, each beachhead touched

        at minutely different times.
No violators, not one. Nobody goes to jail.
Pricking portents like bladders,
we modulate to another key, and run up
        ladders in a stocking to the sky.
—But do not completely forget the string.
It trips, limps, rots, loses threads,

one by one. Lo, it is many things—
        Lanced in Lansing, it jumped the Soo,
froze in the Frisians, and now coils quietly
in the Pacific of your mind, nose to tail.
O beloved, what to do, but keep looking for
        the silver lily beyond the mountains
and shake its golden pollen over our heads.

Nebula through Telescope

Out in the empty darkness so dark it shines,
Where the only vows are accepted, not made,
And even God does not yet know himself,
A yellow flower is tethered, not shying away

Zigzag, but enfeoffed by richest desolations
In a fog where violence hammers, elbowing
Creation out of raw dark matter, not latticed
Or shuttered—nothing jumped up or gilded,

But colliding, rumbling, crashing, yet quiet,
This music by telescope, as a deer in red leaves
Wide-eared and listening. Yet in the begetting
Fires, what calm catastrophe, what cold collusion.

At the End of the Day

I curled up, remembering Mother, Father,
a faraway war, the bayou, its warm, fishy smell,

the moon floating by my window
                like a lost baby tooth,

fiddler crabs, each with one big elbow, leaving
tiny stacks of sand cannon-balls on the shore,

black snakes sunning themselves in the grass,
bright orange lobes of the flame vine

        climbing, taking over the branches
            of live oaks and slash pines,

everything breathing in and out with the tide,
before the first lightning flash of desire—

        before my flame vine caught fire.

Hotel Splendide

    —Is that you, dearest,
    reeking of frangipani?

Men and women
    in handsome linen
    feel the sun's feathers,
              fat canary
sleeping in the transom. Ducks
swim reflections of Alps,
    the Dents de Midi
rushing in, smiling,
           toothsome as aunts.
I, the pretty dwarf in a hood,
    its inner side strewn
with poppies and mandrake root,
           carefully extricate
a small man
    out of my pocket
    and tip him out O so cunning
    on the sidewalk to dance.
Mother and all
the Invisible People
    suck in their breaths reverently
    —and once again
we sweep
    out of fantasy
        into the actual lobby
           of the Hotel Splendide.

Petal, Clay, Ice

I breathe by sun and moon,
               still being chiseled
out of the world's hardening goo—
     you are a submerged island
         of petal, clay, and ice.
How ardently the sea
        embraces islands.
               How eagerly tree-roots
                  tangle and entwine.
—Under this blanket
              of time and space,
embedded
      in such necessity and desire,
              we two still touch.

She Looks Back

to her high school years
and envies her blindness,
her unclosing to everything,
no hopes, no dreams,
but like a dog,
now now now
and she could say she wasted
those days, but she knows
she could use some of that now
—and in her college years,
closing in, choosing this and that,
getting opinions, vain of course,
but always closing here and there,
until now everything is decided,
and she will die an individual—
but sometimes she misses her old
watery self,
swimming like
a transparent jellyfish
in a clear blue sea, back when
she didn't even know
her sting could kill.

How Quickly

The sea must eat its fill—
    a container vessel now and then,
        a swimmer caught in the undertow,
a nautilus shell, one chamber stuck open,
    swept helplessly across the ocean,
        children on the shore,
sailors in war, cruise ships in storms,
    a jet ski zooming away without its rider,
        a tsunami's big gulp.
Well, what of it. We are conceived in water,
    and should be used to hauling it around,
        sloshing, kissing,
taking water in and letting it out.
    The Gulf surges over our heads,
        and the water in us rises and falls
at yon Luna's pleasure. We sink like ships
    and jump like dolphins. Like clouds
        we are wrestled by the wind
into different shapes and destinations.
    When the wind dies, how quickly the sea
        and sky hold hands, and stars
and starfish skinny-dip together in the dark.

Islander

My rowboat rubs against the shore
    and they are there, breathless,

waiting for me, rushing me, those
    who can be consoled by nothing

but the presence of the beloved,
    fugitive as she may be. My people!

I kiss their hands tenderly. They wear
    skirts of palm fronds, palm crowns.

Slowly, I kiss their faces, their eyelids.
    Hammocks stretch between dark pines

lit by flame-vine and white herons.
    —But now we know that I must go—

they push my boat back into the waves.
    I see my mother watching, her arms

encircling the children I did not have.
    See me waving frantically to mine own,

who, in the tremolo of nesting birds,
    live inside the secret of the unseen unsaid,

held and withheld. –Someday, able to bear it,
    I will not leave.

Stairway for a Demiurge

Madam, in the safety of your bed-chamber,
        please ignore the Whore of Babylon
smirking on the sill, draped in sundogs,

        and recline in your velvets, reflecting
on Time and Desire, insatiable lovers
        born from the loveless couplings

of underground newts. —Milady, touch
        your red artery of imagination, your
blue vein of knowledge, your lovely head

        the center, heart a little left of center.
My arms are carrying you up the stairway,
        your yellow hair cascading over me,

far away from this short, painful domain
        of endless possibility and limitation
into my empire of wind, clouds, snow, rain.

The Poetry Reading

Too many ricochets
       & not enough living
babies in this infantry
    Too many glass eyes
taken out, polished
       & pushed back in again
not deep enough in flesh
    never to come back
Nothing squeezed to death
      or blown to kingdom come
by poly-armed consonants
    & eely vowels gargling oil
monsoons & water spouts
       in the ocean air of our mouths
—My green flag with red sunset
   splits, letting the sun
poke its head through
     & anything can happen—
Language lifts her neon skirt
   to expose her dangerous
mouth folding away
      like a map, a bayonet
like origami, like breath.

Le Jardin de Picpus

This garden lies in fine flower,
but there are those who would weed

in busy arbor until every thrust
of life is gone and only buried

seeds remain. The middle position—
thrusting arbor between hedges of roses

and delphiniums on its right and left—
requires most courage. We are not

called to uproot the Vicomptesse
de Noailles rose nor laugh at the gaffer

who digs the trench to dump mangled
products of the guillotine. Beware

the Undoubting. They love to kill,
to point and say, "*tu*, over there

with the spray of dull pollen on your
sullen face—and *vous*, in the upstart ruff

of cursed gold—*You two die first.*"

I Visit my Husband's Grave at the Veterans Cemetery

When the spaceship touched down at 5:20 a.m.,
    how quietly it left, and you, Mistress Moon,

        what do you say, walking quietly across the sky,
and you, stars, who blink and blink, what did you see?

    I want to lie down on the grave, as I've seen others do,
        but the sod hasn't been laid, and there are bird tracks

in the mud—wide open V's with a line down the middle,
    —maybe cranes, symbol of long life. He wanted

        so much to live—that look he gave me, his whole soul
pouring out of his eyes. He died because his body

    said he had to, had to, had to. Some kind of crescendo
        had been reached, like azaleas bursting bloom.

La Vie en Orange

Love conscripted me
into a haboob of windy bangings
        on the door of the universe,
                a fandango in an abyss,
but when I squeezed through
        the hinges of a bivalve,
that enormous orange scallop
            called Spirit and Matter,
                it opened wide
as the jaws of life and death,
and dissolved me like salt
        into a lumpy chowder
thick with stars
            hiding in sunshine.

Woman with a Tree on her Head

That tree grew enormous, as she grew
    Smaller and older, gaining largess,
Even as she waned, cantankerous.

Budding elsewhere, she licked dew
    That trickled its horny bark. She caught
Flickerings of leaves, breathed snow

Into hot lungs—bloomed magnolia.
    All things blossomed in her double sight.
She knew, dying in the double bed,

That tree was hatching an egg in its nest,
    Key in its mouth, moon on its breast—
Flapping its branches, flying ahead.

THANKS to Muriel Nelson, Martha Zweig, Deena Linett, Babo Kamel Edwards, Ann Folwell Stanford, Kathy Peterson, and Anne McCrary Sullivan for the depth of their artistry, discernment and help. And to my family: Lili, Madison, Nate and Jessica, always there, like breathing, like news from the sun.

PATRICIA CORBUS was born in Sarasota, FL, and now lives in Charlotte, NC. She has a B.A. from Agnes Scott College, a Master's degree from UNC/ Chapel Hill, and an MFA from the Warren Wilson MFA Program. She's the author of two poetry collections: *Ashes, Jade, Mirrors*, 2002, and *Finestra's Window*, winner of the 2015 Off the Grid Poetry Prize. She wishes that she could say something true and rare about poetry, but finds it beyond all telling.